ANUSTHA DIARY

ILLUSION

ANUSTHA PAL

ISBN 979-888591027-9

This Book is dedicated to all my well-wishers those who supported me to write this book. I am very grateful for the notion press and my editor who is an important part of this book. I want to thanks

Contents

Contents

Foreword

The author of this book Ms. Anustha Pal, started her work when she was 19. She took her graduated with a Bachelor of Technology in Computer Science and Engineering, which is too Far from writing but she knew and define her writings and poetry at that time making her publish her thoughts and vision in the form of the poetry book. Her parents and people around her inspired her to write what she feels. She inspires people around her from being a beautiful Poet. She wrote amazing books - "Scars" and "Door to my Soul" that are too interesting to Read.

Preface

I am Anustha Pal, Now I have completed seventh semester of B. Tech and my journey take me to this book. This book is soul and I tell everything according to what I feel in few days passed and I hope all the readers enjoy my book. This book contains amazing experiences and story-based poetry that make you feel delight, with rhythm I make these poems sound good to your heart.

Thank you so much for reading!!

Author: ANUSTHA PAL

1. DIARY

When I see my hair,
Curling out on my face
dangles of skirts Are talking,
To my womanhood
Using my body to hold that,
Decent fame for this diary.
When I talk to my notebook
He calls out Mr. precious to be
The president of my diary.
My diary flowing out, like a brook
with a new hook, with
Each turning page.
I become immortal
With every anecdote
of my diary.

How bad and rude
Loneliness is with me.
so Isolated of me and darken parts of me,
then Comes out in my hands
Articles And experiences of my dairy
put Complication my eyes so starry,
perfect angles are at their perfect
Degree.

To measure dwell, people,
Fell into my darkness and into my well.
But they reach their own limits
And dairy is still is my hand,
to rewrite and change

Description:- the poet watching a web series finding the character of a boy Similar to him so she is presenting her views on similarities with him .

2. VIRTUALLY YOU

I start watching a companion
which is parallel to me
Just like a web series, with reality
looking deep into my eye.
My neighbour asked to stop doing
tremendous conversations.
Which I learn from him and
His query.
I ask him, you know you Are just
adorable than I think,
your Body language is not genuine
But still, I am pointing.
When I watch my own web Series,
thrilling and amazing crazy people in it.
I really feel I am just a story and a character
not defined well.
I found nothing else a cup of
Sake and satisfaction which is
Virtual and but still true.
Most of the time my worry And
work are useless, anxiety kicking me hard.
But still, I will never be passionless.
By every time I get my new dates.
And my new journey

To become more incredible
More lovely, to change all the
past, into a future out of a haze.

3. EPOCH

For the Garden of piece,
We are burning everyday.
For others sleep we are
battling every day.
To establishment of
new seeds, we destroy our
Own identity.
Forgiving birth to child,
mother take that pain happily.
In the sake of lush fruit, bud died
Happily.
They say this is naturally but for
Me this is the biggest struggle
Unbelievably.
To get some drops of honey,
Somebody walking miles to get
Nectar.
When country is dying , patriotic
Feelings hold every part and cluster.
My father erase their personality,
to decorate my dreams.
Farmer shedding their sweat,
blood and tears for food
making.

Hey rivers and ocean don't smile
you struggle drop by drop
To maintain alive cores on the
Earth.
A student struggles to make
Give significance of pen.
And police struggle to take
Criminal in the pen.
Lord Shiva drink all the poison
To let people take essence.
This world works on dimensions
of sacrifices.
It will never end.

Description:- the poet write this poem when she is waiting for her two old friends.

4. WAIT

Watching inside from red curtains.
In the smell of the bakery
Under the scorching sun
and Immense heat.
What I am doing is waiting
When I am wandering of things
Too great,
And the thing that rolling
inside my mind is your wait.
With a pageant,
With small talks
I am waiting for two doughy
Norms.
Girls sweet innocent and
full of blossom.
They are just hanging in blue
and Purple.
When they arrived I got (:
Some agitation n excitement.
And then our small talks,
Distribute with some old Memories
of old friends.

And we distribute facts

and love to each.
Takes the slices of pizza
without rapacity n suspense.
And after living in the arena.
We all have a smile on our faces.

5. SCAR OF HINDUSTAN

When some people betrayed our
mother's soul,
Trespassers attacked on the chest
Of our mother India.
We get defeated on our soil.
by our owns.
Getting the peace in death,
this is Indian self-respect.
We waste much dew of our
Bloodshed,
When weapons have seemed
Unavailable,
we make ourselves the weapon of mother
she fights and holds.
Is there is any relationship is possible between stone and flower?
Is friendship of jackal has any probability with King loin,
So how do they defeat us?
We lose because we believe
In respecting everyone,
Atithi Devo bhava is not just our
culture, it's our emotion;
By wearing the dress of emotions
they take
Our wealth and species,

Take our gold and called us
Beggar?
they thought they can make us
poor,
but they have no idea of brilliant minds
India holds,
Friendship with a betrayer,
Is a simile of pocket with a hole.
The golden bird was dying
and that evil heart pouring poison.
Now revenge heart destroy
The shape of the bangle with their
Angle.
Soli of Haldi ghati admiring his
Smile,
now feeling keep and calm,
Cuckoo leaves her melody in sake
of opposing them.
Bonded labour of indigo was
Now free,
We fight without Any violence
With round glasses and fantastic ideas.
The man on the currency note
Make victory.
and leave a message about what victory mean.

6. SILHOUETTE

To be in the imagination
To be in the custom of yours
I discover a world of silhouette
Which appear near this brook.
Flowing out some leaves of
Emotions,
Treasuring and fleeing the
Miniature life and it's magnificence.

Attraction in the world is so
Intense,
And kindness don't really need
This,
But still it resides apart in everyone's
Heart.
Coming up from the brighter side
I am dwelling inside the black,
Not so glorious and my skin is
Black.
Many times I explore my beauty
But enhance by nobody.
Everyone have different shadows,
One silhouette that sun give is
Perfect .

Black is perfect but still people
Disrespect.
Clock is my only hope.
I wait for right time in it.

7. EXPLORE

Watching the grumble
Out of windows going
Inside my paradise.
Hell Healed the blunders
Being living my soul
Alone.
Making the moments of
Comes in life to share,
Crossing the doors of
Inferiority just in a bless.
Loneliness took their space.
Obstacles are the biggest
Factor when you explore .
You are innovative just
Support.
Over the bridges of mind ,
Seal all the impatience ,
Young ladies you just need
Some courage.
Marriage is crucialaspect
That comfort your life.
But this is not the real story
of Your life.
Sometimes parents limitation you

To don't do.
But if you are a real person
So just explore and explore.

8. THE LUXURY CAGE

How did it takes me to
The edge of events,
How gravity falls to
Deflect my curiosity
in my blunts.
Who'sthat stranger
Halted the union from
My body to soul.
How uneasy is to pursue
Smooth luxury of a bird,
If I jumped to live inside
a cage.
A moment which shattered the
Belief of being caged,
Instead of being a dynamic,
WhenVitality is taken In a
Prisontrinket,
This is nothing but theend
Of Meadows which takes you
To life.

9. MEMORY BUS

I try to think about my
Life,
It's everything is very difficult
Because everything brings you
To me.
And I found I am running from
Your images
But like a album they stuck
In my home mind
And slide show of your
Is on replay.
I am running and you album
Is here and there
For being getting away from
You
I stop in front bus stop,
I turn my leg out to go inside
But the moment I stand
I see you.
I hate to tell that my
Opinion is you.

From in sake of running from
You,

I passed my smile to some
Beautiful people
In reply you are stand in their
Back
I smile back this time I having
Tears in my eyes because I loose.
But still my heart is yours.
One day my heart stop this
Game
And I am empty with a void
Heart.

10. BALLAD

When I think about your story
So promising and tangled.
I smell my heart and said
Did you glance that I am turning
And learning.
Greedy greasy people brushing
My story to make it adorable and inspiring.
When a ripe person like me,
Start handing gun in one hand
And knife in other.
So, how can I say that
everything is fair,
My story is empty without
Your craze, without your showcase.
But I become a blender you never
Admire not a glory woman,
In spite of, I am a fire.
Because of that, my story takes bends
I am not submitting, this is not an incomplete
Story,
But also not my story's end.
May be Nothing lefts,
but a crazy women like me make
This story epic.

11. EMPTY MINDS

After getting surplus jolly
Becoming scared n anxiety
Is common
But what a Lonely Planet bring
Out of curiosity of everyone
Thatbelieve us.
Sorry for not having
The fake fateful smile on
My face
Sarcasm has it's own
Beauty I Accept.

The thing which take out
Your soul
And let you stand like a
Death peace.
Your legs tell that you
In that moment you learn
Something about real dog
And Bitch.

12. LETTER

all the moments live in small
Bits,
In the bag of memory holding
Various coins
Sandy memories encompass
Some beautiful moments,
But our life also has some
Raven memories that we rewind,
We run from them,
we wanna escape.
Remote dairy record our every
Gaze.
On a grateful day, it hit the
Door,
Without taking any visiting pass,
A letter falls on the porch with
Some scarlet red blood.
The letter talks About the
Panorama when I am on
the balcony one day,
Watching the road at midnight
with grace and peace.
A stranger commencing
through stary eyes and

addressing something toMe.
That shook my breath,
I feel uneasy it take my
Breath away.
That person wearing a red T-shirt
with some annoying voice,
Calling out something strange
Which I am not aware about.
The letter didn't took me
To his home because he's
A homeless guy.
He lost his parents in an
Accident now he is a mental
Patient with nothing in his
Mind.
His crisis and tear are inside the letter,
In this clever world, there is no
One for his help. I am a ninteen
year old woman,
in this crowdy place
Sorry I ignored you that
Night.
Society having their
boundary
I am allowed to do this
from mine.
I wish at that instant
my father,
Standing at that balcony.

I know surely he helps,
if He will get this
letter.

13. DELETED

There some messages left
Undeleted,
The query is left with this brain
I can't even pretend or figure
What is the next message
going To come,
Some of them will
change the vibes
But one story arrived which
change my Life.

Hello lady!
It's sound fine when
He just begins,
But it becomes a convincing
The story within the end.
Without any known identity
He hook-up that night!
He's trying something unbelievable,
What's this such a mess?
I don't know what is your
Identity,
What still I get distracted.
Without any management

Settlement in that talk.
You are a terrible stranger
Or a wonderfull guy?
You break my flaws, you took
All my night.
You talking sweet like a
Melody
You breathing all my sanity.
He suddenly brought some
Patience and said that
He love my eyes.

I replied suspiciously it
No more work on me bye
Bye,
He broke his silence put some
Music on
He suspiciously answer that I am an illusion, of yourMind.
I say pls stop your jokes
Pls get to the point,
I am not a Queen with beautiful
Face and eye..
Pls don't waste your go for
Somebody else
If you fumble I am not their
To correct.
He say a sentence which I
Never forget until end of my
Life.

That become the reason of
My victory and light.
I kept that sentence in my
Mind as a secret.
That message that
Change my every reason
Of life.

14. LAST PHOTO

Last memory I hold in my
Breath.
The last stage of meeting nectar.
Notion of getting detached
from soul,
Makes my vibes get worried
I take one last picture then
Get our cords lost forever.
I remember your grace,
Yourwardrobe and dresses
The way you get up,
How you feel and take
Up every stress.
Anxious eyes look at the load
Everyday but there nothing
whom to talk and say.....
The that bubble of my dress,
We take the last photo and last
Breathe together.
Your sporty face don't fit in any
Fixture.
We just capture that moment
and smile in that shining light.
It's our last photo and

ANUSTHA PAL

last breathe together

15. LOVE

How are you holding the chunks of
Every glory,
How is your caption is in every
Story,
In your game
There is no Stubborn upset,
There is no incentive
but we celebrate.
Their swirling eyes stubborn
me to drown my haze.
These antelope eyes,
Put my shades and colors on
Sky.
Seven vowels stubborn them
Deep in six stigmas, beautiful
Sound and vibes.
But still, it's a mystery
How you holding chunks of every
Glory
how's your caption
is in every story?
Love allow to count thousand
Stars.
There is stubborn thoughts

that want to make you stay.
In the moonlighting,
In the fragrance of blazer,
Stubborn aliveness take their
Nap
How your name comes in every story.
You are not an anecdote,
you are epic tale.

16. SLIPPERY

The cascade through which I
Got slipped , and fall into pool of anxiety
The curiosity slips ,
that create whisper in my ear
Some slippery floors make us fall
to reach heaven,
But Some of them take us to hell.
I pell-mell my clothes and thought
Which one I deserve, a slippery
Moment tinge on my shirt.
Cloths decide attempts and the surface
It's slippery nowadays.
Opening one button of the shirt is
A style for someone,
Slut for other some people living apart.
In front of needlerelatives, we
Don't take us.
Few special strangersmake their
Life slippery.
Without any intention, we slip
Nobody left then,
your good wishers only stay.
Slippery floor don't believe that
Somebody is not strict,

Even not mention and don't
Believe that, the stream is
Greasy.

Everything slip slops events
Bends
money in the market, make
People depress,
faith in Believe beloved wings,
make stoneHearted people
instead,
Tongue in conversation,
Leading Divorce run.
Step in student, who make
Them terrorist.
Respect of women, just fall
By some stary eyes and short
Dresses.
After crossing this slippery
Floor there is a place we reach
From where nobody can steal
Collyrium from eyes,
Anklet fromfoot,
Shade in afternoon
In the griefahhh!
Wow! s in the joy,
Slippery floor make you
Feel stress but the lesson
It teaches is always best.

17. DAY

**in this poem poetess wants you to*
Saying to keep motivated and how to make your day by doing
*Stuff**

Sitting up in a Imperial ,
Breathing in the
Gesture of your pace,
Dreaming all day long
The lovely Summer rain.
Picture out the
Colours,
Take the belly dance,
Flow your body in the
Rhythm,
Make fun, gestures and
Laughs.
Sticking your snap
On the wall,
Drink in the cold
Fog,
But left nothing to smell.

Sniff your perfume
Make drama with your

Pal ,
Try to drive in the sky
Let some hair to shiver.

Google something out,
Explore something new,
Open your hands and
Just make something
Out
Which tell about you.

18. CHANGED

The tool I had never seen
Whole life,
It's your stare.
That gazes me all night.
Summary and history of
All your all night out.
You ratified all the lusty
Nights.
Annoying and disturbing
Now Without any surprise.
Curiosity kills the cat and
Rats running in my mind
all the time.
Misfortune is now everywhere
And failures catch up with my time.
I try to survive but it brings me
Empty.
There's no space like me anywhere.
Pranking and uncovering
every Night.
Without thesestary eyes,
I just found a empty night
With nothing inside.

19. RESIDENTS

You make resident
In me.
To help you I drop me
Down from my dark shadows.
I am a spirit,
Who live in fired
Desires and despair left
In a bag like me unworthy.
The purpose is living in the
Ripped jeans , you Wore.
I left me in pieces
You never encounter,
Napping in the lap
Of others.
You are talkative, but Dumb for me.

20. PERCENTAGE OF LIFE

The stardust of my
Charismatic eyes,
Plucking fruits in jolly
Summer,
To be in mirror action,
Sketching my reflections.
U still design you
But like a monkey.
For the sake of getting something
New, I jump into the lake of
Curiosity.
To be peaceful non-dramatic
Don't speak but your
Nervousness says,
I have some fear and
My Beauty is in gravity
and always stay.
Real beauty is in Acknowledgement.
I left behind some,
Glory and true lights.
See the fabricYourcloths
they Remember you in you
In your sweat and fire.
And at very last our fabric

, beauty, curiosity ends with
Clock hands we become
Intentionless.

21. STRONG RIBBONS

Dusk is not the color
of my grace.
Haze used to vanish from
My face.
There is nothing like this feeling
Which make blood rose,
in my fleck brain,
Even inside my real fame.
This is not just a cozy day,
It is not for which you set for,
It is a wave of an eclipse,
To praise and to raise for.
Taking the sip of the wine,
Catherine & best endorsement
to Gaze.
This time when gazes don't work,
Be reckless, this will help you
To play your day.
Continue to be glossy,
When there is nothing left,
Shady and scarlet waves,
then limits,
Design Your path,
it's a time to say.

It's the eternity to be a
real men.

22. RELENTLESS

Everything supposes to be alive,
capture some journey.
every eye meeting commence,
nobody hearts to beats
alive things make you love again
and again
that's how every avenger will continue.
we all pioneers of peace, always remain
calm
we are warriors for peace.
war continues lifelong.
that's strangely we live on...
non-voilence and misbehaving remain
at the slope of a straight line.
the ugly truth is coming like a flood
play, pause, and then rewind.
the people who are waiting for
revenge, play red hands-on coast
west.
we will write and share our humor,
we also need sarcasm, it's not bullshit
its something real.
we believe in our god just like a
plant of tulsi ,

that purify our body and soul.
we ring our bells of temple daily,
we believe in pure sounds like
our cultural music.
we are the puppets hanging on the
shakspere plays,
playing fine in every role.
our mothers working hard to make
bricks and stone a home.
everything which suppose to be alive
have some journey, believe in this
relentness and come out of probability.

23. HATE

Hate the hate which makes
You hate
Hate that words which make me
Blade
Hate that blood that flows through my
Arms in misery due to wait
Stupid creatures stupid wave which
Hate the honest review that you make
Courtesy that you give to your arms
For being brave in the Patriot feelings that
I usually hate
But families in this world have a crazy soulmate
Which make everyone feel amaze
I m the part that nobody use to hate ,
Because this earth define me with the silence
Which everyone can't make
But if you genuinely ask there are reasons
That let me hate the pages that i wrote in the
World imaginary that i make.

But still my life have parts that make.

24. SUN

Magnificent people r along
My way,
Now I perceive like I can brush out all that sympathy
my friend give to me and all the dirt u throw
On me.
A time comes when u are known
To every person.
N globally a piece of news will
arrive that
"All hurty n violate attempt r
Not underestimated ".
N for being too much disrespectful with me,
For being wrong with me,
I take u under the unity
Of infinite lights. Under
The master of warmness
In chilly hot wind,
Inside all that alluring crowd.
every 24 hours of yours you'll agonize
Not from fire but by my aggression.
I'll stop your smears
For touching me at that
Angle at which I'll not even
Bend me.

N finally I'll make you deceased.
Without missing your single blood drop.

25. Bucket

My mind is a bucket with holes
pipelining that I have done wide break my soul.
I am trying to be superstitious
for my goals
My behaviours have issues which you can troll.
An astonishing piece in the eyeballs
And mermaid-like me, leave the water
for another floor.
I try to carry my life in this green grocery bag,
But the skinny dress doesn't go
with my shoes.
Try to look enthusiastic all the time,
But I am from my soul too slow and cool.
In the end, being mindset is too freaky and careless
and I stand on the stool of pride to tell
I am so cool.

Thank you so much for reading this book...

Printed by Libri Plureos GmbH in Hamburg,
Germany